At a Glance™ Series

DVD and Lesson Book

D0504045

DVD Fretboard Theory

Written by Joe Charupakorn and Chad Johnson
Video Performers: Doug Boduch and Marcus Henderson

ISBN: 978-1-4234-9486-7

HAL•LEONARD®
CORPORATION
7777 W. BLUEMOUND RD. P.O. BOX 13819 MILWAUKEE, WI 53213

Visit Hal Leonard Online at
www.halleonard.com

Table of Contents

INTRODUCTION

Welcome to *DVD Fretboard Theory*, from Hal Leonard's exciting At a Glance series. Not as in-depth and slow moving as traditional method books, the material in *DVD Fretboard Theory* is presented in a snappy and fun manner and will help you learn important soloing strategies in virtually no time at all. Plus, the At a Glance series uses real riffs and licks by real artists to illustrate how the concepts you're learning are used by the masters. For example, in *DVD Fretboard Theory*, you'll learn riffs and licks from classics like Dire Straits' "Sultans of Swing," Carlos Santana's "Oye Como Va," and The Beatles' "Day Tripper," to name just a few.

Additionally, each book in the At a Glance series comes with a DVD containing video lessons that correspond to the printed material. The DVD that accompanies this book contains four video lessons, each approximately 8 to 10 minutes in length, that correspond to the topics covered in *DVD Fretboard Theory*. In these videos, ace instructors Doug Boduch and Marcus Henderson will show you in great detail the CAGED system, which visually organizes the guitar neck into familiar shapes so you'll never have any problem staying in key no matter where you are on the fretboard. You'll also learn about the modes and how they're used in real songs—not just in theory—as well as learning how to find the "good" notes used to harmonize melodies. As you go through *DVD Fretboard Theory*, try to play the examples first on your own, and then check out the DVD for additional help or to see if you played it correctly. As the saying goes, "A picture is worth a thousand words," so be sure to use this invaluable tool on your quest to mastering the mysteries of the fretboard.

FRETBOARD NAVIGATION

Having a command of the guitar's fretboard allows you to find any note when you need it. This lesson is all about fretboard navigation and requires that your guitar be in standard tuning: E–A–D–G–B–E. Alternate tunings change the shape of chords and scales, so they'd require a modification of the system we'll study today.

You'll need to spend a little extra time to digest the materials in this lesson if it's new to you. However, this will be time very well spent and once you absorb the material; it will forever change the way you see the guitar.

Five-Pattern or "CAGED" System

As you might know, the same notes exist in more than one place on the guitar. These recurring notes create a system of five patterns that we use to map the fretboard. Each pattern corresponds with a moveable left-hand position used for chords, scales, and licks. The backbone of each pattern is the root—just one note—so we'll focus on that. Once you can instinctively locate the root in any shape and any key, you'll never have a problem playing in any key anywhere on the neck. But this will take some hard work; the upside is that it will definitely pay off.

We'll start with using the five CAGED patterns to find every instance of the note C on the fretboard and then we'll see how the same system applies to any note. "CAGED" is an acronym for C, A, G, E, and D major chord shapes, which will be our reference points. The system maintains that, by knowing where the root of each shape is located and understanding how these chord shapes interconnect when played with a single root, you can play in any key and in any position on the neck. Follow along with the DVD, then make your own diagrams on blank sheets of paper to help commit the patterns to memory. You'll use this for the rest of your life, so it's definitely worth the trouble to write it down.

 On a blank sheet of paper, make a big six-string fingerboard diagram with at least fifteen frets on it like this.

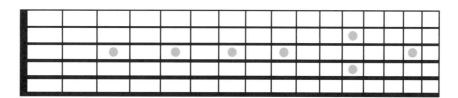

Set your pick aside and keep your pencil handy. We'll just pluck the notes with our fingers for the time being.

Pattern One

Pattern One shows us the lowest available C notes on the guitar: at fret 1 of the second string and fret 3 of the fifth string. Fret the notes with your first and third fingers. Notice that your fingers are two frets apart. This lesson is all about visualizing notes on the fretboard, so be really mindful about these note locations and shapes.

 Mark these two notes with the letter C on your diagram, then circle the two together and label as Pattern 1.

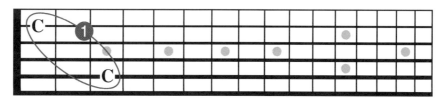

4

Notice the Pattern One Cs intertwined in these songs. (Note: In "Landslide," a capo is placed on fret 3, causing the song to sound in E♭. If you want to play along with the original recording, be sure to capo at the third fret.)

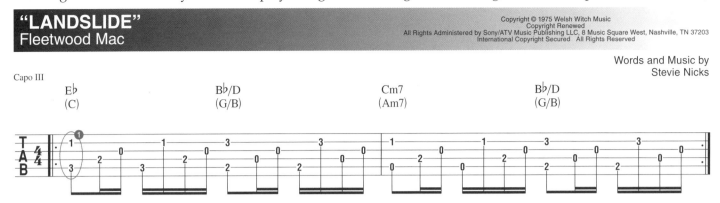

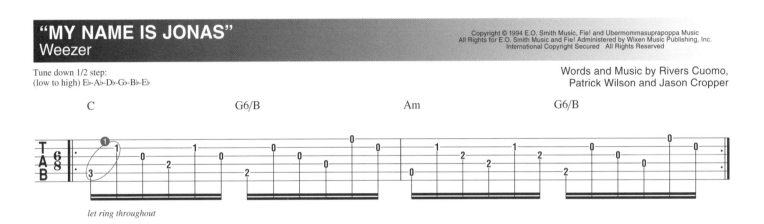

Pattern Two

Now lift your third finger and replace it with the first finger on string 5, fret 3. Place your third finger on the third string at fret 5. This is Pattern Two of C. These are the same C notes in terms of sound, only in a higher position on the neck. Your fingers are two frets apart again.

Mark the note and circle Pattern Two on your diagram as on the DVD.

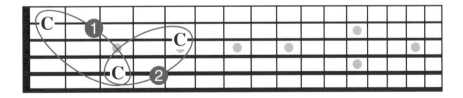

In the pre-chorus of "St. Anger," Metallica hits the two Cs of Pattern Two in their octave riff.

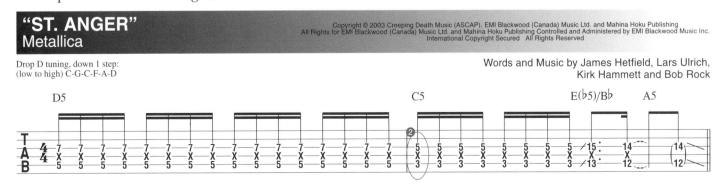

As does Radiohead in their song "Creep."

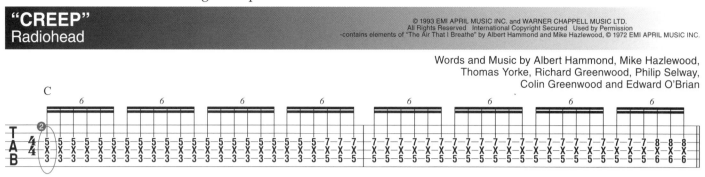

Pattern Three

Again, move up the neck, this time lifting your third finger and replacing it with your first finger on string 3, fret 5. Now place your pinky finger on string 1 at fret 8. This is Pattern Three. Notice that there is a three-fret distance from the lower C to the higher one in this pattern.

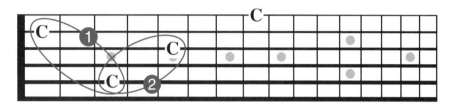

The chorus of Weezer's "My Name Is Jonas" takes this shape and uses it to melodically ascend. Try to identify the name of the notes as you play this rather than just thinking of it as a finger shape.

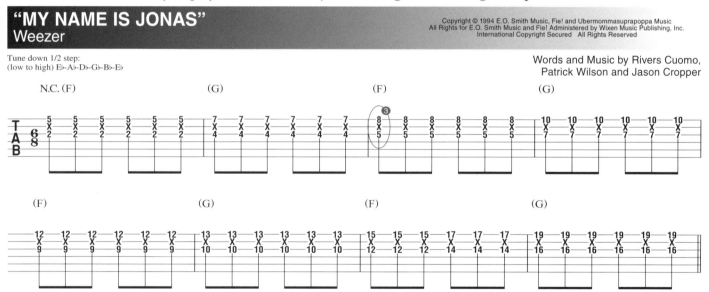

This pattern also includes another C that we can play on the low E string. It's not necessary to play all three notes in the pattern at once. We just need to know where they are. The note on the low E string is always on the same fret as the same note (two octaves higher of course) on the high E string.

Mark the two new C notes on the first and sixth strings in your diagram, then circle Pattern Three and label it.

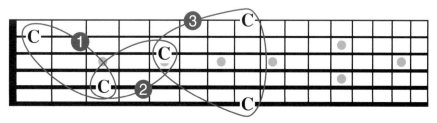

Pattern Four

For Pattern Four, we move up again, placing our first finger on the C at string 6, fret 8. We also use the first finger for the C on string 1 at fret 8. The higher C in Pattern Four is on string 4 at fret 10. Hold it down with your third finger while you alternate the other two Cs. Pluck these three notes only.

 Now mark your diagram with the new note, circling and labeling Pattern Four.

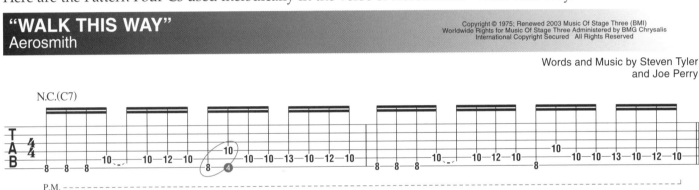

Here are the Pattern Four Cs used melodically in the verse of Aerosmith's "Walk This Way."

"WALK THIS WAY"
Aerosmith

Words and Music by Steven Tyler
and Joe Perry

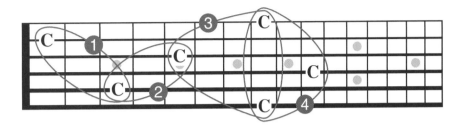

Pattern Five

 For Pattern Five, we again move our first finger to the higher spot in the previous pattern and add the higher C on string 2, fret 13. Pluck these two notes, then mark your diagram at string 2, fret 13, and circle and label Pattern 5.

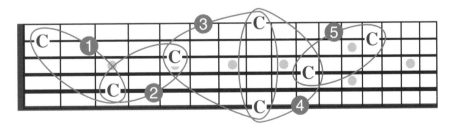

Patterns two, three, four, and five are often used to play octave runs and may be familiar to you. However, while these shapes may be common, it's important to always be aware of the name of the note you're playing rather than just thinking of it in terms of the physical shape.

We checked out "My Name Is Jonas" for Patterns One and Three. The harmony part to the chorus of the song uses the Pattern Five shape to catch the octaves.

Tune down 1/2 step:
(low to high) Eb-Ab-Db-Gb-Bb-Eb

Words and Music by Rivers Cuomo,
Patrick Wilson and Jason Cropper

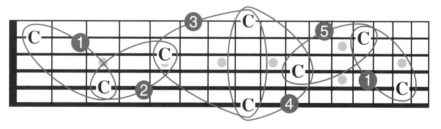

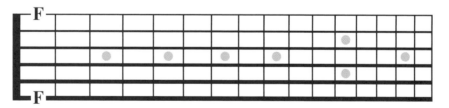

Pattern One at Fret 13

The high C in Pattern 5 is twelve frets higher than the one we started with. Now place your first finger on this note and your third finger on string 5, fret 15. The five-pattern system is starting over here and continues until the guitar runs out of frets.

Though we could continue into infinity, we've just marked the last diagrams with another instance of Pattern One so you can see how they overlap.

Five Patterns of F

For a little more practice with this concept, let's now find every F on the fretboard. The lowest Fs are one fret above the open E strings on strings 6 and 1.

These are followed by an F at the third fret of the fourth string.

You may recognize this as Pattern 4, which was at the eighth fret when we were working with C notes.

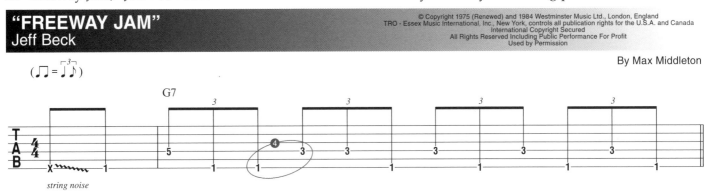

In "Freeway Jam," Jeff Beck uses the Pattern Four Fs to create a rhythmically interesting phrase.

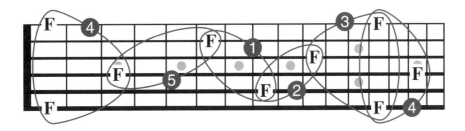

By Max Middleton

string noise

The five patterns always occur in the same order. That's one of the reasons the system is so valuable. Once we've found that we're in Pattern Four, the rest fall into place, starting with Pattern Five at the third fret.

In "Couldn't Stand the Weather," Stevie Ray Vaughan plays Pattern Three of F; can you relate this shape to the others?

"COULDN'T STAND THE WEATHER"
Stevie Ray Vaughan

Tune down 1/2 step:
(low to high) Eb-Ab-Db-Gb-Bb-Eb

Written by Stevie Ray Vaughan

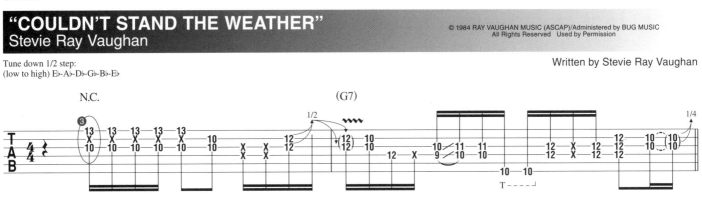

Watch the DVD and note how all the patterns "imply" common chord shapes. Practice using the five patterns to find all occurrences of one different note a day for a few minutes each day until this system becomes familiar and intuitive. Draw one new fretboard diagram each day to reinforce your knowledge. You can keep this kind of practice very short, but be consistent until you've got it down!

CAGED LICKS

Through the years, many systems have been devised to help guitarists visualize the fretboard and thus easily transpose their favorite licks to different keys. One of these is the CAGED system. We learned the basics of this system in the previous lesson; now let's use it to create some more riffs and licks.

C-Shape Major Scale

Our first lick is based on the open C chord shape's major scale pattern. To avoid using open strings, we'll play it one octave higher at the twelfth fret. This way, the pattern will be immediately "transposable." The circled note in the diagram indicates the root.

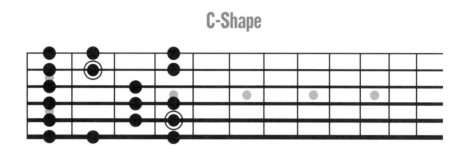

C-Shape

Thinking in relation to chord shapes, can you visualize the shape of the C chord webbed into this lick from Bob Marley's "No Woman No Cry?"

"NO WOMAN NO CRY"
Bob Marley

Words and Music by
Vincent Ford

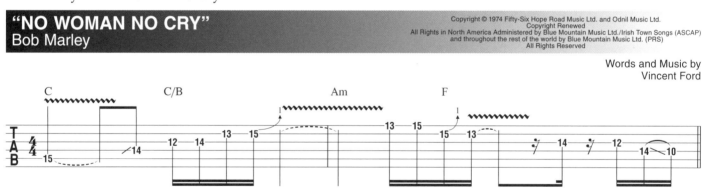

This lick comes right out of the Curtis Mayfield and Jimi Hendrix school of R&B double-stop chord soloing. It works great as a closing phrase for a solo or interlude section. The trick here is getting the double-stop fingerings down, so take your time.

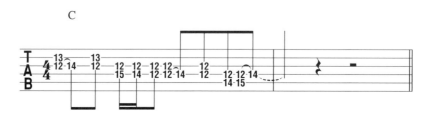

A-Shape Major Scale

Our second lick is based on the A-shape major scale.

A-Shape

This shape is the basis for some of the riffs played in Living Colour's "Cult of Personality."

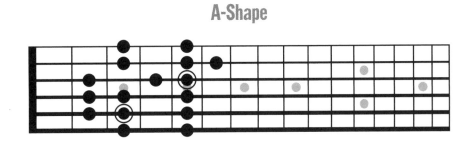

Here's a bluegrass lick in the style of such legendary pickers as Tony Rice and Norman Blake. While most bluegrass licks are played in open position, guitarists sometimes venture up the neck using closed position shapes. The A-shape scale pattern, particularly in the key of C, is a popular one, as it is basically an extension of the open-position C shape. It's kind of like the open-position C shape but with open strings replaced by fretted ones on the lower adjacent strings. Try and imagine both shapes overlapping to get an idea of how the different shapes connect as you move up the fretboard.

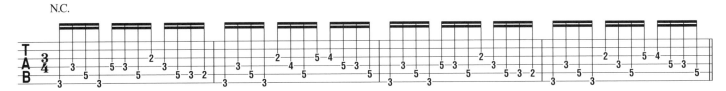

G-Shape Major Scale

Next is the G-shape major scale pattern, which looks like this, in the key of C. Try to visualize an open G chord shape contained in this fingering.

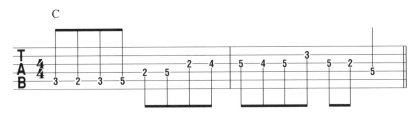

G-Shape

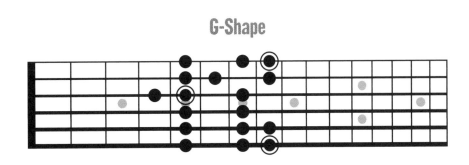

This lick is a blues-rock phrase in the style of Aerosmith's Joe Perry. It's based on the G-shape pattern, but with the addition of a ♭3rd and ♭7th. The addition of these "blue" notes (flatted versions of crucial chord tones) is a common blues gesture.

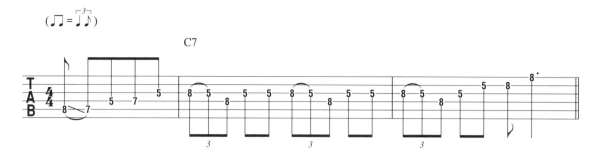

In "Walk This Way," Joe Perry really milks the ♭3rd and ♭7th, in addition to using the major 3rd. Once you learn the basic scale shapes, it's easy to add the "blue" notes.

"WALK THIS WAY"
Aerosmith

Words and Music by Steven Tyler
and Joe Perry

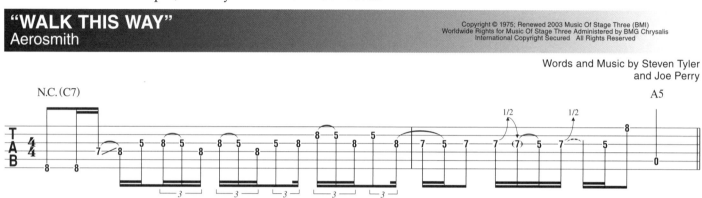

E-Shape Major Scale

The next major scale pattern is based on the E-shape chord form. This shape is usually one of the first major scale shapes taught because it's easy to visualize in relation to the open E chord or its related barre chord shape. Here it is in the key of C.

E-Shape

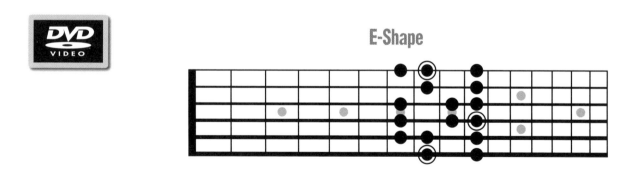

In Cream's "Sunshine of Your Love," watch how the opening riff is derived from the E-barre chord shape, which is actually played later in measures 5 and 7 (here it's in D). This riff also makes use of added blue notes like the ♭5th and the ♭3rd.

"SUNSHINE OF YOUR LOVE"
Cream

Words and Music by Jack Bruce,
Pete Brown and Eric Clapton

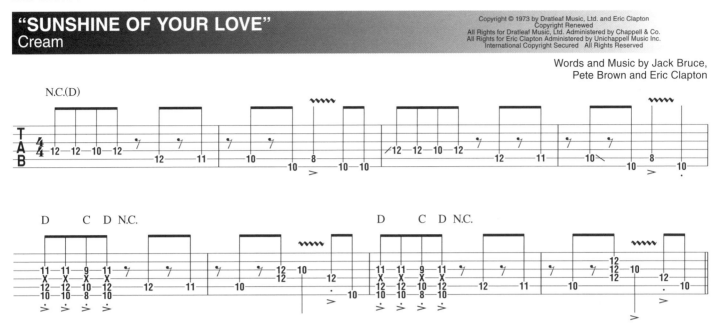

The E-shape pattern is a popular one also for rockabilly, blues, and country-rock players because the common E-barre chord "grip" is right under the fingers. This lick is inspired by Mark Knopfler's ever-melodic and tasteful bag of treats. Strive for an even, steady attack to create a rolling, ostinato effect. Take special care not to rush the hammer-ons and pull-offs.

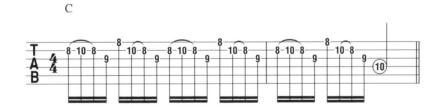

You can hear Knopfler doing these kinds of runs in the outro solo of "Sultans of Swing."

"SULTANS OF SWING"
Dire Straits

Words and Music by
Mark Knopfler

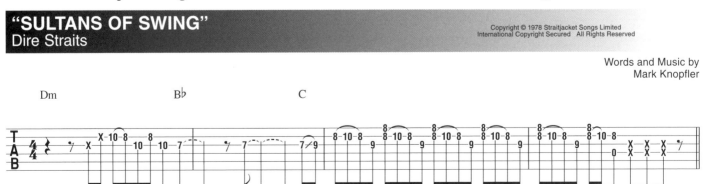

In "Crossroads," Eric Clapton uses the E shape played in A (on the fifth fret) to generate this bluesy lick. The shape is conducive to mixing in both the bluesy ♭3rd and the major 3rd because both notes are easily accessible; Clapton does just that.

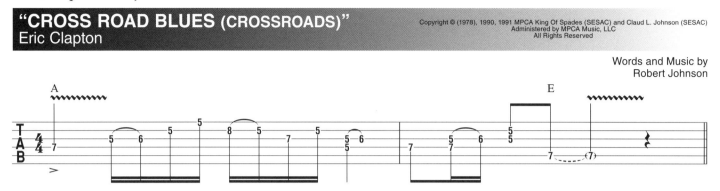

"CROSS ROAD BLUES (CROSSROADS)"
Eric Clapton

Words and Music by
Robert Johnson

D-Shape Major Scale

The final major scale shape in the CAGED system is based on the open D chord shape. Here it is in C.

D-Shape

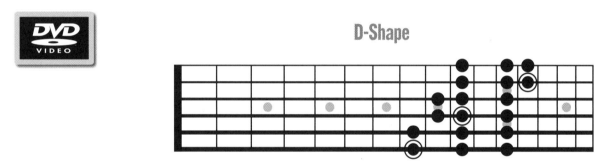

Slash used this shape to generate the intro riff to "Sweet Child O' Mine." Try to envision the D-chord shape as you play this riff.

"SWEET CHILD O' MINE"
Guns N' Roses

Tune down 1/2 step:
(low to high) E♭-A♭-D♭-G♭-B♭-E♭

Words and Music by W. Axl Rose, Slash,
Izzy Stradlin', Duff McKagan
and Steven Adler

N.C.

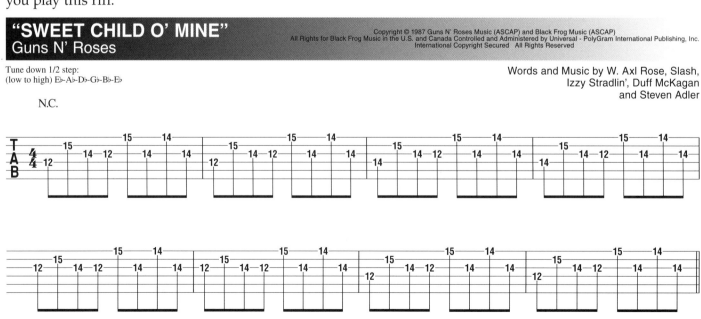

If you're a studied shredder, you may recognize the embedded D-shape major scale pattern as one of the "three-notes-per-string" fingerings used for straightforward scalar runs and even string-skipping licks. But it's not just for shredders. The shape also presents a fresh change of pace for country guitarists, as shown with this legato-fueled country lick, which ends with a Nashville-approved pedal steel bend to a C major dyad. Make sure you keep a steady rhythm, and don't rush the pull-offs.

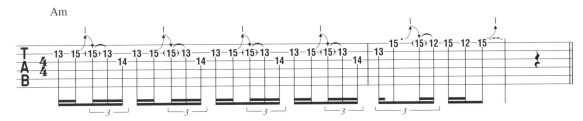

Relative Minor Approach

The CAGED system is based on major chord shapes and their associated major scales. But most rock, blues-rock, and blues licks have their roots in minor scale shapes. What's a guitarist to do?

Use the *relative minor* approach. Without getting into lengthy detail, each major scale has a relative minor equivalent, which contains the exact same notes, only starting on the 6th scale degree. We'll study the relative minor is greater detail in the Modal Soloing lesson starting on page 18.

C	D	E	F	G	**A**	B
1	2	3	4	5	**6**	7

In the key of C major, the 6th scale degree is A. So, if you play each of the five CAGED scale shapes in the key of C starting on the note A instead of C, you'll have the five relative minor scale patterns.

In this next section, we'll look at some licks using the two most popular shapes.

A Minor Based on C-Shape Pattern

The first minor lick, inspired by the great Jimmy Page's blazing repeating passage in the "Stairway to Heaven" solo, is based on the relative minor scale of the C-shape pattern. You might recognize this as a common minor scale pattern with its root on the fifth string.

This lick has a fairly tricky triplet rhythm, but the driving force is its overall feel, so don't sweat strict counting.

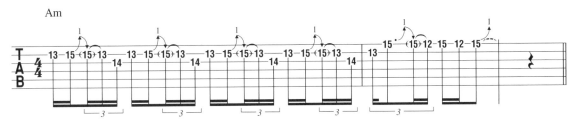

In his solo on "Top Jimmy," Eddie Van Halen mixes this shape with the E blues scale for a lethal legato run.

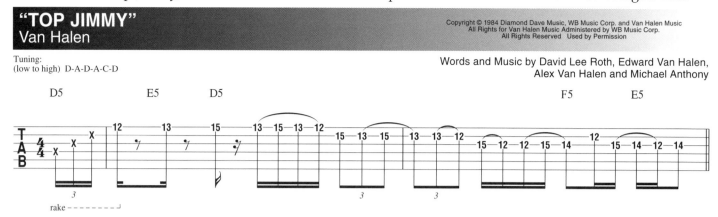

"TOP JIMMY"
Van Halen

Words and Music by David Lee Roth, Edward Van Halen,
Alex Van Halen and Michael Anthony

Tuning:
(low to high) D-A-D-A-C-D

Of course this shape isn't only for playing fiery licks. Check out how the Ventures used it in the opening of "Walk Don't Run." Here it's played in the open position and employs open strings.

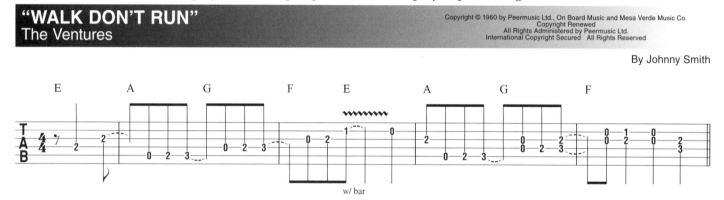

"WALK DON'T RUN"
The Ventures

By Johnny Smith

A Minor Based on G-Shape Pattern

The second minor lick, a stock run in A minor, is culled from the relative minor of the G-shape pattern. You might recognize this as the common sixth-string rooted minor scale shape.

Because the minor pentatonic scale is contained in this shape, we can easily start off with a typical blues bend before grabbing the notes specific to the A minor scale (like the sixth-fret F note on the second string).

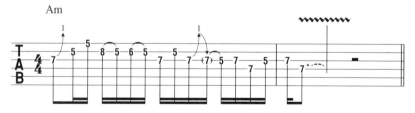

Randy Rhoads took this idea one step further and also added notes from the blues scale in this run from "Crazy Train," based on F# minor.

"CRAZY TRAIN"
Ozzy Osbourne

Words and Music by Ozzy Osbourne,
Randy Rhoads and Bob Daisley

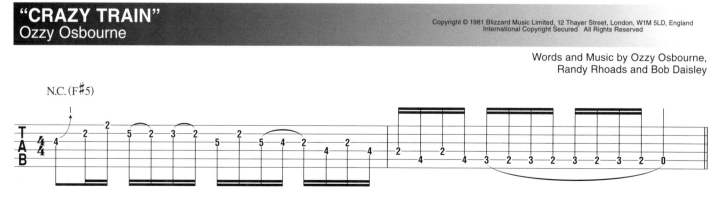

Connecting the Dots

For our final examples, we'll look at scale sequences that span several CAGED scale patterns. Both of these sequences are the types of scale runs you might hear in a hard rock or shred setting.

The first one, in C major, uses a descending six-note sequence that climbs up the fretboard one pattern at a time. Although it will most likely be difficult, use alternate picking here and practice the lick with a metronome to make sure you're playing it accurately.

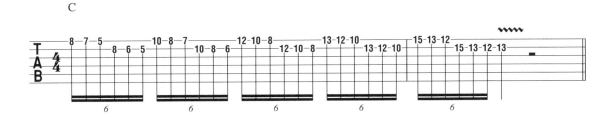

This lick, in E minor, uses an ascending six-note pattern spanning several CAGED scale shapes on its way up the fretboard. Like the previous lick, alternate picking is the order of the day here.

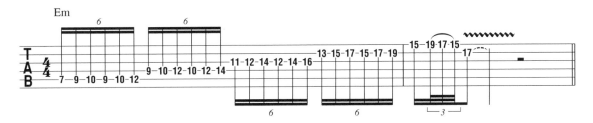

Check out the fretboard-melting ascending run at the climax of the solo in Whitesnake's "Here I Go Again."

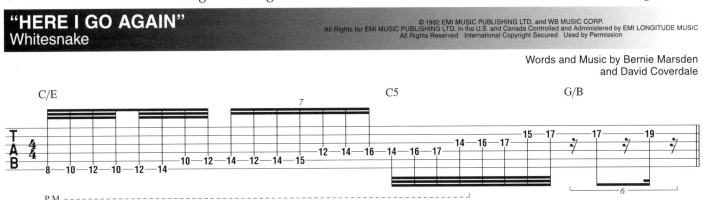

"HERE I GO AGAIN"
Whitesnake

Words and Music by Bernie Marsden
and David Coverdale

That concludes this lesson on licks based on the CAGED system of fretboard mapping. Be sure to work out your own licks using each of the scale patterns—major and minor—of the CAGED system, and as you play through your favorite songs, look for other licks based on these shapes as well. Further, try to create phrases that connect two or more of the CAGED patterns to truly supercharge your fretboard navigation skills.

MODAL SOLOING

If you're growing tired of the standard major, minor, and pentatonic scales, then it's time to discover the wonderful, wide world of modes. In this lesson, we're going to shed some light on the modal mystery and learn some pretty cool licks in the process.

Decoding the Modes

Modes are one of the most misunderstood concepts in all of guitardom, but they don't need to be. It's really pretty simple, as long as you understand some basic theory.

There are seven diatonic modes (don't be scared off by their fancy names):

1. Ionian
2. Dorian
3. Phrygian
4. Lydian
5. Mixolydian
6. Aeolian
7. Locrian

Parent Major Scale Approach

There are basically two ways to look at modes. The first is to relate them all to a parent major scale.

 Let's play a C major scale, which is spelled C–D–E–F–G–A–B.

C Major Scale

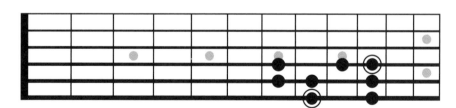

Ionian = Major Scale

Aeolian = Relative Minor

Guess what? You just played your first mode. The Ionian mode is the same as a major scale. By the same token, the Aeolian mode is the same as the relative minor scale. So, C Ionian is a C major scale, and A Aeolian is the A minor scale.

Assuming you know the major and minor scale, we don't need to look at them.

Now, if we play those same notes of the C major scale and treat the second note, D, as the root, we're playing a different mode: D Dorian.

D Dorian

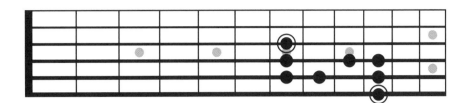

We can continue this way throughout the whole C major scale. Treating the third note, E, as the root, we get the E Phrygian mode, and so on.

So, the seven modes of C major then are:

C Ionian

D Dorian

E Phrygian

F Lydian

G Mixolydian

A Aeolian

B Locrian

This is a very academic way of looking at the modes, because, without some kind of context, they're all pretty much going to sound like the C major scale.

 Check out the DVD and see if you hear any shifts in tonality. Basically, it all sounds like C major, right?

Separate Scales Approach

If we view the modes as separate scales, each with its own intervallic formula, then we're able to get some context.

Ionian Mode

For example, the intervallic formula for the major scale, or the Ionian mode, is:

Ionian Mode

1–2–3–4–5–6–7

 It's the standard formula by which we measure other scales. In C, this looks like:

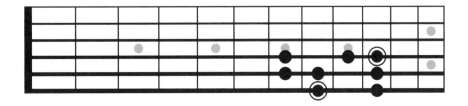

Since this scale contains a major 3rd, it's said to be a major mode. By altering this formula, we end up with other scales or modes.

The major scale (Ionian mode) is not especially common in rock guitar solos, which are often based on the minor pentatonic scale. But in some cases, there's no better choice than the major scale. The solo in Pat Benatar's "Hit Me with Your Best Shot" opens with a perfectly executed run from the E major scale.

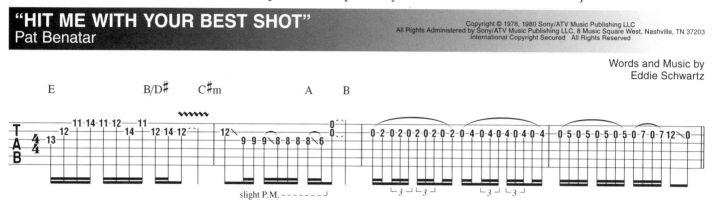

Randy Rhoad's solo on Ozzy Osbourne's Beatles-esque "Goodbye to Romance" is derived from the D major scale.

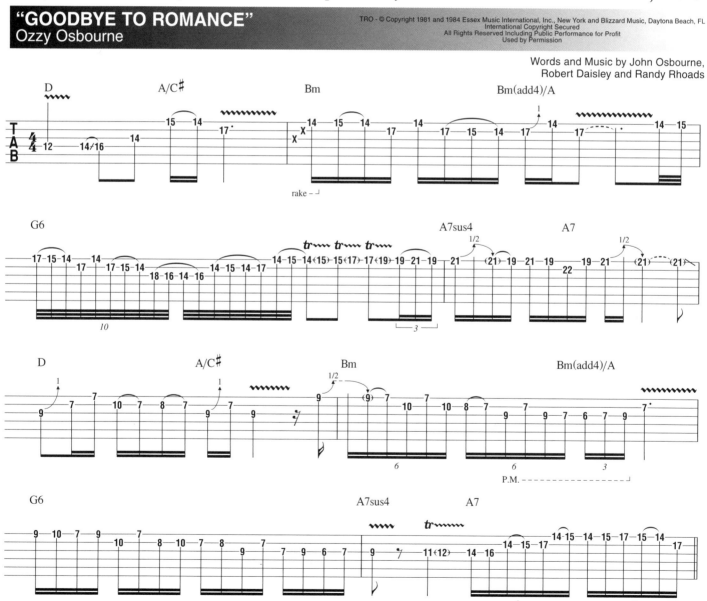

Dorian Mode

The formula for the Dorian mode is 1–2–♭3–4–5–6–♭7. If we flat the 3rd and 7th degrees of the C major scale, we'll end up with a C Dorian mode. Here's a common fingering for C Dorian around eighth position:

C Dorian

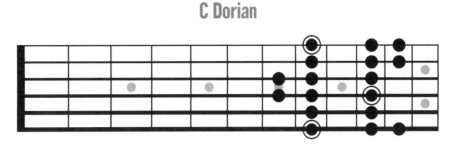

Since this scale has a minor 3rd, it's a minor mode. So, over a C minor chord, we could use the C Dorian mode as an alternative to the C minor scale.

Let's say you have this Cm7 groove:

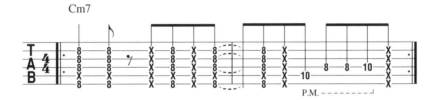

Here's a C Dorian line you might play over it. This lick has a jazz-fusion touch.

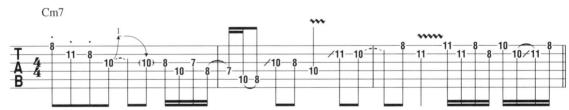

Carlos Santana's guitar style often prominently features the Dorian mode. Here's an excerpt from "Oye Como Va" based on the A Dorian mode.

"OYE COMO VA"
Santana

Words and Music by
Tito Puente

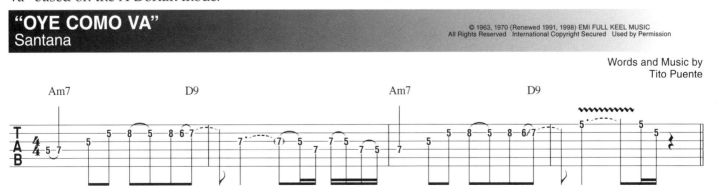

Here's more of a straight-ahead rock lick using C Dorian over the Cm7 vamp.

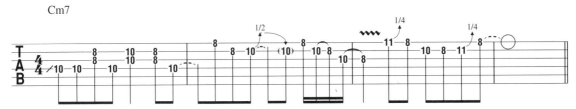

Kansas employs the A Dorian mode for a hard-rockin' riff in "Carry on Wayward Son."

"CARRY ON WAYWARD SON"
Kansas

Words and Music by
Kerry Livgren

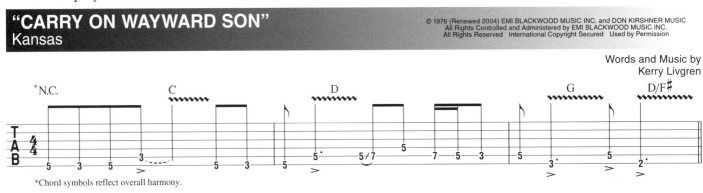

*Chord symbols reflect overall harmony.

Mixolydian Mode

If we refer back to our C major scale and just flat the 7th degree, we'd get C Mixolydian, because the formula for Mixolydian is 1–2–3–4–5–6–♭7. Here's a fingering for C Mixolydian:

C Mixolydian

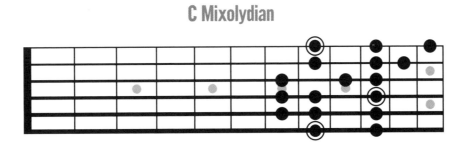

Since this has a major 3rd, again, it's a major mode. But more specifically, it's a dominant mode because of the ♭7th degree. So you can use it over a C triad, or it's perfect to use over a C7 vamp, like this:

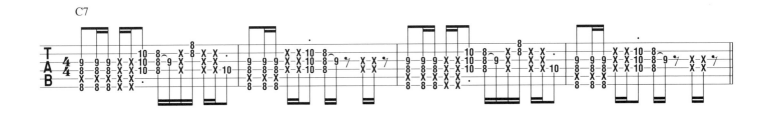

Here's what the C Mixolydian mode sounds like over that vamp.

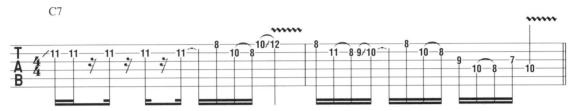

Or how about something a little funkier?

The opening to "Jump, Jive an' Wail," as played by The Brian Setzer Orchestra, makes use of the B♭ Mixolydian mode. The B♭ triad figures prominently into this riff, but the 6th (G) and ♭7th (A♭) give the riff its Mixolydian flavor.

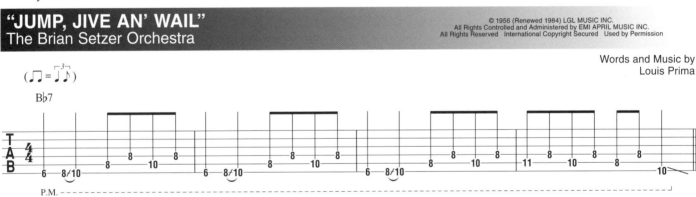

"JUMP, JIVE AN' WAIL"
The Brian Setzer Orchestra

Words and Music by
Louis Prima

Since the Mixolydian mode can sound bluesy, often times the ♭3rd blue note is added into Mixolydian riffs to add to that effect. The intro to the Beatles' "Day Tripper" slips in a ♭3rd just before beat 3; otherwise it's all E Mixolydian.

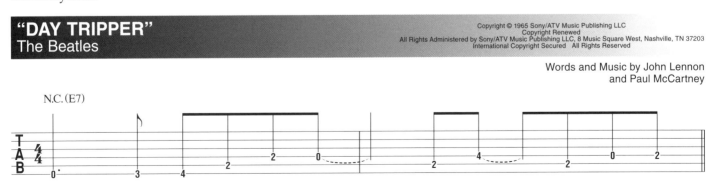

"DAY TRIPPER"
The Beatles

Words and Music by John Lennon
and Paul McCartney

Lydian Mode

If we take a C major scale and raise the 4th, we get the C Lydian mode, because the formula for Lydian is 1–2–3–#4–5–6–7. Here's a fingering for C Lydian.

C Lydian

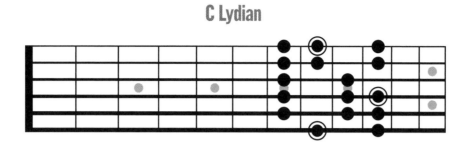

Again, we have a major 3rd, so it's a major mode. Lydian is very bright and dramatic and used in a lot of film scores. Since it has a major 7th as well, it's an alternative for soloing over major 7th chords. But it's not recommended for use over dominant 7th chords, which contain flat 7ths.

Let's work with a simple rhythm pattern based on Cmaj7:

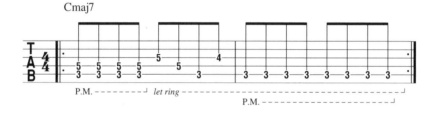

Here's an example of a C Lydian line over that pattern:

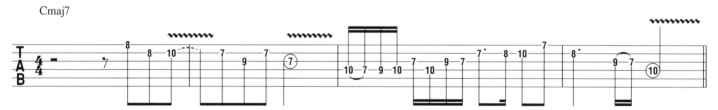

It gets your attention, huh? Let's check out another lick using Lydian.

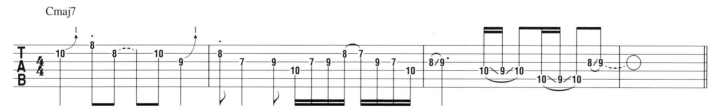

By exploiting the major 7th (A) and ♯11th (E—♯11 is another way to refer to the ♯4) over the B♭ chord, Marty Friedman brings out a Lydian flavor to this lick in one of his many solos in Megadeth's "Hangar 18."

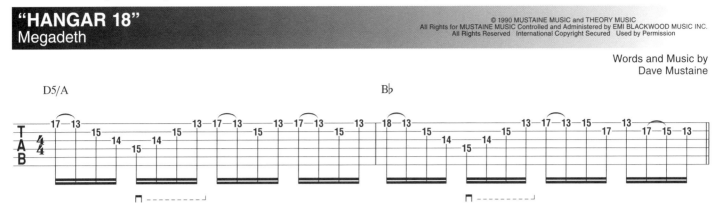

We covered Dorian, Mixolydian, and Lydian first, because they're the most commonly used modes, besides Ionian and Aeolian of course, which you already know.

Phrygian Mode

Another one you occasionally see is Phrygian; its formula is 1–♭2–♭3–4–5–♭6–♭7. Here's C Phrygian.

C Phrygian

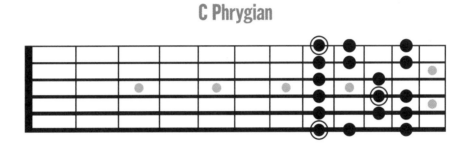

With a minor 3rd, this is another minor mode, but since it contains a ♭2nd, it's a much darker one. You'll hear this one used in metal often. Say you have a C power chord riff, like this one:

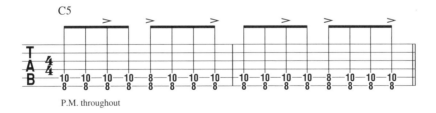

We can use the Phrygian mode to create a slightly evil sound.

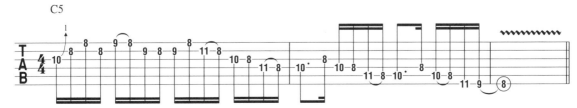

In the ominous "Mr. Crowley," Randy Rhoads takes a quick run based primarily on D Phrygian.

Copyright © 1981 Blizzard Music Limited, 12 Thayer Street, London, W1M 5LD, England
International Copyright Secured   All Rights Reserved

Words and Music by Ozzy Osbourne,
Randy Rhoads and Bob Daisley

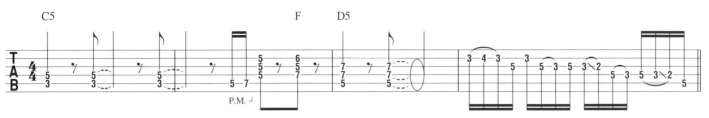

Locrian Mode

Since Locrian contains a ♭3rd *and* a ♭5th, it's technically a diminished mode, or, more specifically, half diminished. Because of this, it's rarely used outside of soloing over minor 7♭5 chords, which aren't too common outside of jazz. However, the ♭5 is commonly heard in metal, so the Locrian influence should not be overlooked.

To be thorough and cover everything, here's a fingering for C Locrian:

C Locrian

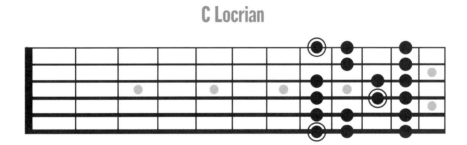

Hopefully, this has helped you understand modes and how they are commonly used. The next time you're jamming along with someone, try pulling out one of these licks and turn a few heads! Good luck.

HARMONIZING LEAD LINES

Few things in rock are as electrifying as a dual-guitar solo. It's fun, it adds an extra level of complexity to your music, and hey, the fans love it! In this introductory lesson on harmonizing lead lines, we're going to look at how to create your own show-stopping harmony-guitar parts.

Diatonic Harmonization

For starters, it's imperative that you use diatonic intervals when harmonizing your lead lines. This simply means that all of the notes in the harmony line should be in the same key as those in the melody line. Otherwise, it will sound wacky like you're in the Twilight Zone.

Good thing you learned how to get around the neck while staying in key in the previous lessons! That knowledge will come in handy for this lesson.

Diatonic 3rds

The first interval we'll examine is the diatonic 3rd. Western harmony is based on the concept of stacked 3rds; thus it should come as little surprise that the 3rd is the most popular harmonization interval. To take your first step into harmony guitar, let's harmonize the C major scale in 3rds.

 Here's a popular C major scale shape commonly used by rock players. Notice the boundaries of this shape; does it look familiar? Remember Pattern Three from our Fretboard Navigation lesson? This is it.

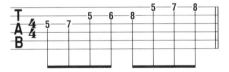

 To harmonize the scale in 3rds, simply start on the root, C, and count up two whole steps, to E, and then just play the notes of the C major scale, from E to E.

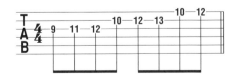

 Check out the DVD to hear what both parts sound like together.

You might recognize that sound as the basis of such classic guitar harmonies as Steely Dan's "Reelin' in the Years."

"REELIN' IN THE YEARS"
Steely Dan

Words and Music by Walter Becker
and Donald Fagen

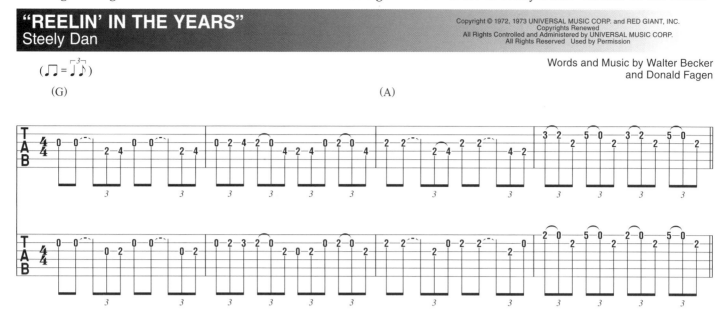

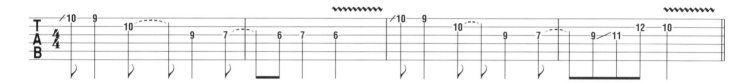

Ratt's "Round and Round" and the Allman Brothers' "Jessica" are other famous examples of the harmonized guitar sound. Here's a phrase in the style of "Jessica." It's in the key of A major and is played at a tempo of 128 beats per minute.

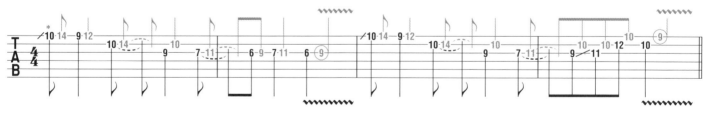

Now, to harmonize that phrase up a 3rd, simply find the 3rd above each note of the melody line, staying diatonic to the key of A major, and then play the resulting harmony line over the melody, using the same rhythm.

*Melody notes shown in black, harmony notes shown in gray.

If you're thinking to yourself, hey, I think I heard a 4th in there, you're right. Whenever we came to an E note in the melody, rather than harmonizing it up a 3rd to G, we took it up an additional half step, to A, for a more consonant sound. This is because G is also the major 7th of the underlying chord, A, and we didn't want a jazzy major 7th tonality in this rock phrase.

Unfortunately, there's no general rule of thumb for this type of substitution. You'll just need to use your ear to avoid uncomfortable note pairings, or notes that rub awkwardly against the underlying chords. Play through the notes that are available in the key and you'll definitely find one that works.

Harmonizing Down a Third

So far, we've shown you how to harmonize a melody line by going up a 3rd. You can also harmonize by going down a 3rd. Here's how to do it.

 Using the C major scale as your melody, start by counting backwards two steps to A. Watch the DVD for a demonstration.

 Then play the notes of the C major scale, from A to A, while a second guitarist or backing track plays the C major scale, from C to C.

You can hear this kind of harmonization in the solo of Cinderella's "Nobody's Fool" and, more famously, in the interlude of Boston's "More than a Feeling."

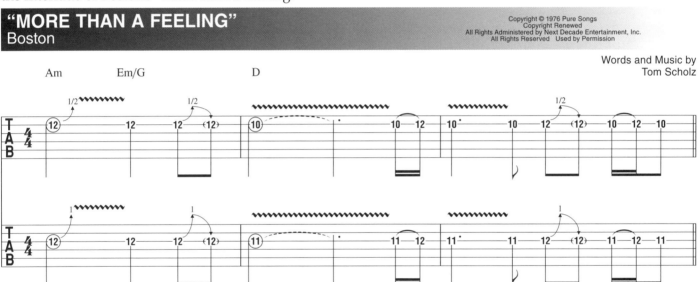

"MORE THAN A FEELING"
Boston

Copyright © 1976 Pure Songs
Copyright Renewed
All Rights Administered by Next Decade Entertainment, Inc.
All Rights Reserved   Used by Permission

Words and Music by
Tom Scholz

Here's a sample phrase in G major, harmonized down a 3rd, inspired by that phrase from Boston.

 First, here's the main melody line.

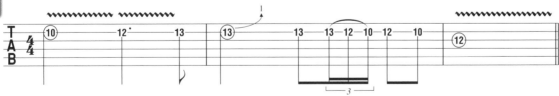

 Here's the harmony down a 3rd, except that we've chosen to end the phrase down a 4th, for a more consonant rock sound. Check out the DVD to hear what both parts sound like together.

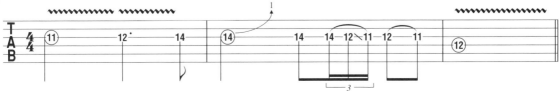

Harmonizing with Sixths

After 3rds, the next most popular harmonization interval is the diatonic 6th. When harmonizing in 6ths, the melody is generally the higher-pitched line of the two. This means that the 6ths-based harmony line can also be viewed as inverted 3rds. That is, instead of just going up a diatonic 3rd to create the harmony line, you go up the 3rd, and then drop that note down an octave, resulting in a harmony line that is a diatonic 6th below the melody.

 To demonstrate, we'll harmonize the E minor scale down a 6th. Here's a popular E minor scale shape.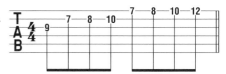

 And now, from the root, E, count backwards five steps to the diatonic 6th, G. Follow the DVD if you're not sure here.

 Then play the notes of the E minor scale, from G to G, over the original E minor scale. Check out the DVD to hear what both parts sound like together.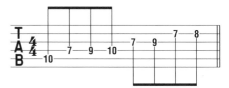

A textbook example of this type of harmonization can be heard in the secondary theme to Iron Maiden's metal classic "The Trooper."

"THE TROOPER"
Iron Maiden

Words and Music by
Steven Harris

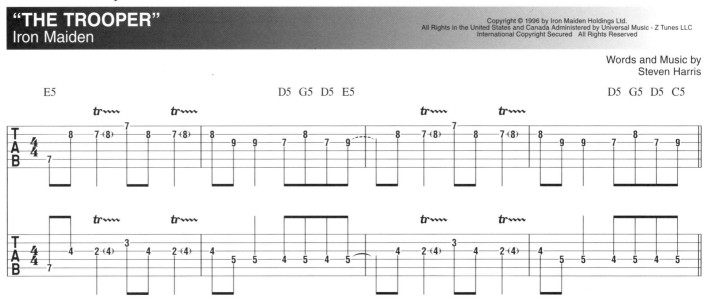

Here's a legato rock example in the key of E minor inspired by the 6ths harmonies of Maiden guitarists Dave Murray and Adrian Smith.

 First, here' the melody phrase.

 And here's the harmony line, down a 6th.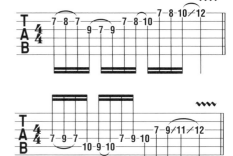

 Check out the DVD to hear what both parts sound like together.

Perfect Intervals

The perfect intervals comprise 4ths, 5ths, and octaves. Because neither octaves nor 5ths hold much musical intrigue for longer harmonized lines, these two intervals are best used for punctuation—or as a third harmony part on top of 3rds or 6ths—to fatten up the overall sound. Additionally, you can substitute 5ths for awkward-sounding 6ths.

That leaves us with the perfect 4th. Earlier, we used 4ths in place of awkward 3rds, but this interval can also be used as a basis for harmonized lines. Perfect 4ths are particularly effective for harmonizing pentatonic-based rock and metal lines. For example, the primarily pentatonic intro to the classic "Smoke on the Water" is harmonized as 4ths. Because perfect 4ths can played as one-finger dyads on all adjacent string sets except the G and B string set, the "Smoke on the Water" intro is played by one guitar.

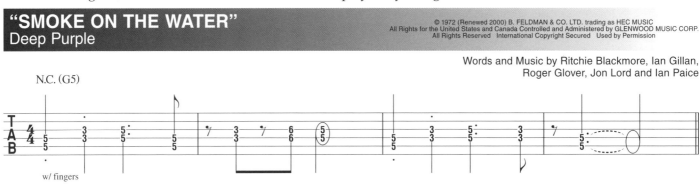

Words and Music by Ritchie Blackmore, Ian Gillan,
Roger Glover, Jon Lord and Ian Paice

Here's a one-octave E minor pentatonic scale in rocker-friendly twelfth position.

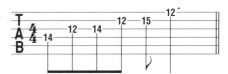

And here's the harmony up a 4th. The DVD demonstrates what both parts sound like together.

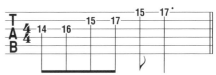

The Scorpions' Mattias Jabs and Rudy Schenker are masters of harmonization. Check out the intro harmony solo in their hit, "Rock You Like a Hurricane," which features harmonies in 4ths and 3rds.

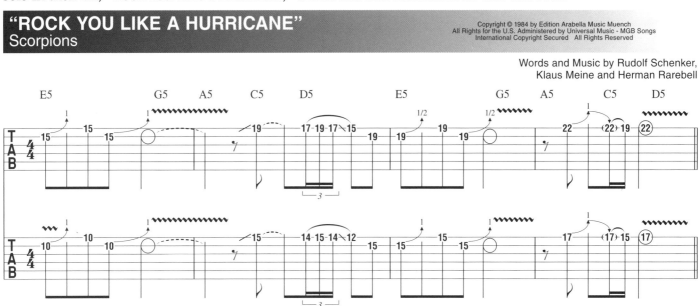

Words and Music by Rudolf Schenker,
Klaus Meine and Herman Rarebell

Here's a harmony line inspired by "Rock You Like a Hurricane."

First, here's the melody line, which is based on the E minor pentatonic shape we just went over.

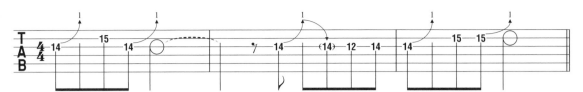

And here's the harmony up a 4th. The DVD demonstrates what both parts sound like together.

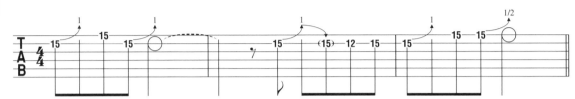

Well, folks, that concludes this lesson on harmonizing lead lines. We hope this has inspired you to further explore the idea of incorporating harmonized lead lines in your own music. In addition to the songs and bands mentioned in this lesson, be sure to check out such artists as Metallica, the Eagles, Molly Hatchet, and Avenged Sevenfold to further hear these concepts masterly applied. And remember, sometimes two notes are better than one!